# this book belongs to:

_____

*and I attract what I desire.*

# 01 law of attraction

The ability to shape your reality

Life is a collaboration between you and the universe

Introducing the law of attraction

The law's powerful history

It's not philosophy, it's science

What the research says

The power of energy, vibration, and frequency

# 02 369 manifestation

The magic of manifestation

People who know its potent power

Manifestation don'ts

Manifestation dos

Sculpt your life

Nikola tesla and the 369 method

How to use the infinite power of 369

Ways you can use the 369 method

Why gratitude is your secret weapon

96-Day 369 manifesting worbook

96-Day calendar

03   your manifesting toolkit
―――

>   Positive affirmations
>   Manifestation quotes
>   Your manifesting toolkit

04   conclusion
―――

# contents.

The Universe is Listening

# the ability to shape your reality.

*'What you can visualize in your mind, you can also hold in your hands.'*

You bought this book because **you understand the power of manifestation.** You know the infinite possibilities your thoughts have over the universe and their ability to transform desire into reality.

You may not realize now, but **the book you currently hold is a tool to attract your deepest desires, wants, and aspirations.** If you're willing, this book can guide you through the process of manifestation, teaching you about its influence and how you can harness this power in your life.

The 369 method is the most dominant manifestation tool, and this book clearly outlines how you can use its potency.

**The ability to shape your reality lies in this book. Use it and watch your life change.**

**Life is a collaboration between you and the universe.**

It gives you exactly what you need when you need it. And what you can visualize in your mind, you can also hold in your hands.

It's not philosophy, it's physics. Given that you are merely energy and everything around you is energy, if you match the frequency of what you want – it will come to you. And when you make a decision or have a thought, the universe conspires to make it happen, giving you a reality aligned with what you focus your attention on.

Imagine thoughts like seeds and attention like water. The more attention you give something, the faster and stronger it will grow, and what you focus your energy on will manifest in your daily life.

**Being what you desire is the key to getting what you desire.**

... life is a
collaboration
between you
& the universe.

Introducing...

# law of attraction.

**All humans have felt the Law of Attraction in the works.** But you may be more familiar with its other names: gut feeling, the power of positive thinking, prayer, The Secret, science.

The same law governs the power of these things.

It's a blend of spirituality and physics – it influences everything we do. At its simplest, the law says that you will attract exactly what you believe. **Your thoughts become your reality.**

And it doesn't matter whether you believe in this philosophy or not. **The Law of Attraction impacts your life every day, regardless.**

The pattern is simple. If you receive an envelope in the mail and believe it to be a bill, chances are it will be. Perhaps you felt the weight of disappointment and financial pressure before you even pulled the letter from its envelope. The sight of the severe-looking bill merely confirms it.

But what happens if you expect the best? If you expected money, a reward, or a heartfelt letter from a loved one? If you'd felt the physical rush of excitement and the physical surge of joy as you peeled back the envelope?

**Like attracts like. Energy matches energy.**

The Law of Attraction is a magnetic and mysterious force that some believe to be magic, others believe to be science. The truth is – it's both.

*'At its simplest, the law says that you will attract exactly what you believe.'*

# the law's powerful history.

There is nothing new-age about this law – it is older than humankind. You'll find it littered throughout history, evident in religion and literature. Buddha said, **"all that we are is a result of what we have thought."** And William Shakespeare wrote, **"nothing is unless our thinking makes it so"**. Dial back thousands of years, Greek Philosopher Plato wrote **"likes tends toward likes"**, in 391 BC. He recognized the fundamental law of this philosophy.

But the term Law of Attraction wasn't born until the 1800s when Russian occultist Helena Blavatsky – co-founder of the Theosophical Society – wrote about it in 'The Secret Doctrine'. Helena, well-known for her spiritual gifts, spoke of humans' ability to sculpt their own lives and turn ideas into reality.

More than a century later, this movement fed into Rhonda Byrne's bestselling book 'The Secret' in 2006. Filled with gripping insights into the power of thought, it became a global sensation that changed lives around the world.

# it's not philosophy, it's science.

Most of us feel the Law of Attraction instinctively. When you stew in stress and negative thoughts, things tend to get worse. When you expect good things, good things seem to happen.

But there is nothing imagined about it. It's science. The way we think can rewire our minds, with decades of research supporting that. There are still mysteries around how it works, but we know it does.

*'... spoke of humans' ability to sculpt their own lives and turn ideas into reality.'*

# what the research says.

Neurology studies suggest visualization can help predict better futures in those that practice it. Some studies even suggest that visualization can change the brain.

A large body of research supports affirmations as a psychological aid. They can help people heal from trauma, boost wellbeing, enhance performance, and shapes better outcomes.

Some of our brains' neurons' mirror behaviors we witness, so it feels like we're doing the same thing. Our brains copy our surroundings. Mirror neurons help us to induce mirror responses in the people around us. So, if you display happy, energetic behaviors, others will mirror them. This supports the philosophy of people's energy vibrating on a high or low frequency.

A team of Korean scientists found those who practiced positive thinking led significantly more satisfying lives. Their focus on the good only pulled more goodness. Quite literally, people can attract positive experiences and outcomes through their thinking.

# the power of energy, vibration & frequency.

Manifestation master Nikola Tesla famously said that

> *"If you want to find the secrets of the universe, think in terms of energy, frequency, and vibration."*

Because everything is made from tiny moving molecules that you cannot see, that's simply fact. Every tree, person, and piece of furniture you see is made from the same vibrating matter. You can't see it, but it's moving to align with its surrounding energy. Your thoughts influence these vibrations. Every thought triggers a sequence of reactions— a domino effect. A chain of tiny, unseeable movements impacts the other vibrating matter – from people to food – around you.

We've all felt the sway of vibrations before. Have you met someone and felt 'off'? Sensed energy that made you want to leave?

Or has someone held a magnetic pull over you? Energy or chemistry you can't help but want to be around?

Chances are, the frequency of your vibrations aligned.

Those vibrations are also why you're much more comfortable around people who mirror your mood. You're attracted to negative people when you're feeling down, and you want to be around people who share your happiness and excitement when you're in a good mood.

But you can change your vibrations by attuning yourself to the present through meditation, nature walks, breathing, or listening to frequency music.

By doing this, you harmonize your vibrations with your surroundings. **And that's the sweet spot – it's where the magic happens.**

*'... you can change your vibrations by attuning yourself to the present.'*

# the magic of manifestation.

Manifestation has traditionally been treated as one of two extremes. Either a magical, witchy mystery or a series of mundane platitudes such as "the power of positive thinking" and "careful what you wish for."

But science is helping to reveal and validate the power of this ancient practice. Research is allowing us to dust off old prejudices and approach the phenomena with fresh eyes. Manifestation and the Law of Attraction is something humans have always half understood. We instinctively know our thoughts matter; we just haven't known how much. The practice transcends cultures, backgrounds and circumstances. And it's our most precious tool.

Because the universe operates on an algorithm. In the same way Facebook, Instagram or TikTok keep showing you more of the content you interact with, the universe does the same. It doesn't matter whether you were watching and commenting because you love or hate the content. It only recognizes that you are interested and paying attention. It's the same with your thoughts – the more you feed your thoughts, the stronger the ripple effects are.

The beauty of manifestation lies in its abundance. It works when you take time to feel what it will feel like to see your dreams manifest.

Pause to imagine the rush of joy you'll experience after seeing your name published or see the first $1 million in your business account. Bask in the glow, the gratitude, the happiness.

**And it will happen. The only question is when and how.**

# people who know its potent power.

**Manifesting is your superpower.** Have you ever heard people say they expected the success of their future? Knew they would rise to the top? In interviews, many celebrities and well-known success stories echo this sentiment.

Princess Diana knew her life was going to be extraordinary. She once said,

> *"I knew that something profound was coming my way".*

It was an unintentional manifestation – while she may not have methodically practiced manifesting, her thoughts and beliefs were powerful enough to impact the trajectory of her life.

Others are purposeful. It's no coincidence that many household names swear by the practice. It has shaped some of the most well-known and successful people of our time.

Academic powerhouses Albert Einstein and Henry Ford famously used manifestation to turn their ideas into realities. Einstein believed in the pull visualisation has over people saying, *"it's not philosophy, it's physics"*.

Will Smith, Oprah Winfrey, Russel Brand, Kanye West and Lady Gaga are all successful people who swear by the power of manifestation. Will Smith, influenced by 'The Alchemist' by Paulo Coelho, has fervently spoken about transforming dreams into realities through manifestation.

Meanwhile, Oprah Winfrey, who grew up poor, has become a household name, destined for the history books. She became the first self-made, black, female billionaire.

These celebrities are all different people, doing different things. But they all claimed power and control over their thoughts. **They focused on turning the thoughts and ideas once limited to their head into their reality.**

*'... transforming dreams into realities through manifestation.'*

# manifestation don'ts.

Don't be half-hearted. Think big and ask for what you want with your chest.

Don't expect anything to happen overnight. It could happen, but don't expect it.

Don't expect anything to fall into your lap. You can't expect to win the Lotto if you've never bought a ticket. You can't expect to land your dream job if you don't apply for it.

Don't be too vague. Rather than focusing on "getting rich" or "getting a job", manifest your dream job or the amount of money you see in your bank account.

Don't pretend always to be happy. Be grateful and consistent, but feelings and hiccups are natural.

# manifestation do's.

Do manifest what you desire wholeheartedly.

Be clear on what you want. Use simple, active, and clear statements for your manifestation. Rather than saying "I want" use statements like "I have" or "I am".

Put pen to paper. There is power in writing things down again, and again, and again.

Trust that it will happen. Those negative thoughts will lower your vibrations if you begin to worry that it hasn't happened yet. Feel your excitement and anticipation.

Do focus on what you're grateful for. Like attracts like – by focusing on appreciation for what you have and what you will soon have, you'll attract more.

# manifestation do's.

*... continued*

Focus on raising your vibrations. Go for nature walks, write about what you're grateful for in a journal, listen to frequency music, meditate.

Work for it. It's a myth that you can cast your wish, and the universe will take care of it. If you want it, you must take action.

Become what you want to be. Want to be wealthy, content, successful? The key is believing that you already are.

Be kind to yourself. Manifestation shouldn't be a painful grind. Lean into your power and honestly believe in the things coming your way.

The Universe is Listening

# sculpt your life.

**You can attract anything into your life – love, money, career success.** While the same overarching guidelines apply, you should approach each slightly differently.

**Manifest money**
_____

**So, what are you really asking for?** You're not asking for money to see the zeros in your bank account or hold a stack of paper bills. You want it for your dream house, to pay off debt, to go on holiday.

When you're manifesting money, focus on what it would feel like to have enough money to achieve that dream. Visualize signing the deed to your dream house, watching the figures in your bank account move out of overdraft.

**Manifest love**
_____

The secret to manifesting romantic love is not wedding your thoughts to a specific person. Instead, **focus on particular traits and details you want in your partner.** Write down those traits and keep revisiting them. Feel what it will feel like to have a person that embodies those traits around you.

## Manifest a career

-----

**Decide what you want and become intentional with your thoughts.** Think about how it will feel to have reached your goal. Instead of thinking about how far you have to go and how unhappy you are in your current situation, feel excited by your dream job.

## Manifest a family

-----

Trying to get pregnant and start a family is something that has ended in hurt for some. Because of that, people often dwell in fear and anxiety. The trick to combatting that fear is affirmations and visualizing the details of your future. **Write empowering affirmations.** Try "my body is designed for my bab" and "my body is bringing life into the world". Visualize your baby's clothes, what it will feel like to feed your infant, the smell of the top of their head.

## Manifest health

-----

For tip-top health, focus on **gratitude for your body** and how grateful you are for the body and mind you will soon have. What it will look like and feel like. Bless your water before drinking it – you can speak affirmations into it. When you drink your morning coffee or tea, visualize the power and health it gives your body.

# nikola tesla & the 369 method.

**If manifestation is the art, 369 is the ultimate tool that will help you create your masterpiece.**

Throughout his life, genius Nikola Tesla was obsessed with the three "magnificent" numbers and the magic they hold. The 19th-century engineer and inventor, who many believe created the 369 method, said those numbers hold "the key to the universe." Tesla would walk around the block three times before entering his building, and he only stayed in hotel rooms with numbers that could be divided by three.

So, why 369?

───────

**The power of these numbers is rooted in complicated mathematics and human history.**

When studying circles (360 degrees), Tesla found that no matter how many times you divided one, the outcomes would always be 3, 6 or 9. If you double one, then two, and carry on, you can create a pattern in which 3, 6 and 9 are the only numbers missed — a sequence that has been called a flux field.

Three is also a significant number throughout human history. Ancient Greek philosophers regarded three as a number that embodies wisdom and harmony. And in religions such as Christianity, humans honour trinities such as the Father, the Son, and the Holy Spirit.

Yet, we can't fully explain the pull of these numbers. Tesla felt they possessed a sacredness, a divinity.

The number 3 is said to align people with the universe, while 6 symbolizes strength. Lastly, 9 is the number of release and healing. Together, the frequency of these numbers is sacred. **By channeling this sacredness, the results are magnificent and life-changing.**

*'Together, the frequency of these numbers is sacred.'*

# how to use the infinite power of 369:

People are often surprised by the simplicity of this method. But it's consistency and conviction to your belief that can make it life-changing.

**It involves intentionally manifesting three times in the morning, six times at midday, and nine times in the evening for 96 days.** This can be done in your head, though there is much more power in putting pen to paper. While you're doing so, focus on what it will feel like to get what you need.

This book has a workbook for all 96 days, meaning you can actively participate in shaping your life and manifesting what you want. Use the book to hold you accountable and attract your deepest desires.

# ways you can use the 369 method:

Decide on your manifestation and commit to it.

Write or speak in the short phrases in the present tense. Use active language like "I will, I am, and I have."

Be consistent. To make sure it works, set a daily alarm as a reminder to manifest in the morning, middle of the day, and evening.

Keep raising your vibrations. If you feel doubt and negativity lowering your frequency, focus on raising it to better align with your goals. It is a vital yet often overlooked part of manifestation.

Write your manifestations when your vibration is high, so try going for a run or having a wonderful conversation with a loved one before.

Don't be surprised if your dreams come earlier or later than you hoped or expected. The universe doesn't operate with the same timing as us. But trust that it will happen at the perfect time.

**Commit to using this method for 96 days and watch your life transform.**

# why gratitude is your secret weapon.

**Your body doesn't know the difference between an experience or a thought.** It really doesn't, and science supports this. We don't need an external event to happen to feel gratitude. We can think, and our whole nervous system changes in an instant.

Some studies even go as far as to say that those who practice gratitude for ten minutes a day strengthen their immune system by 50%.

When you practice gratitude, your body believes that something favorable is going to happen or has happened. It elevates your energy, lifts your vibration, and leaves you in a state of readiness to receive. It is the priming of your soul.

If the Law of Attraction has taught you anything, it's that you attract and resonate with your emotional state. The universe serves you what you are thinking about, feeling, and being. So, if you can stay in a place of gratitude, powerful things will happen.

That is why the workbook in this journal leaves space for practicing gratitude right before you write your manifestations. The mere act of thinking and writing what you are grateful for will lift your frequency and help attract what you desire. Use gratitude as your secret weapon.

*'If the Law of Attraction has taught you anything, it's that you attract and resonate with your emotional state.'*

The Universe is Listening

# where focus goes, energy flows.

## today

I am grateful for

### 3
Morning

01

02

03

Date

# 6
## Afternoon

01

02

03

04

05

06

# 9
## Night

01

02

03

04

05

06

07

08

09

The Universe is Listening

# where focus goes, energy flows.

## today
I am grateful for

## 3
Morning

01

02

03

Date

# 6
## Afternoon

01

02

03

04

05

06

# 9
## Night

01

02

03

04

05

06

07

08

09

The Universe is Listening

# where focus goes, energy flows.

## today
I am grateful for

|  |
|---|
|  |

## 3
Morning

| |
|---|
| 01 |
| 02 |
| 03 |

Date

# 6
## Afternoon

01

02

03

04

05

06

# 9
## Night

01

02

03

04

05

06

07

08

09

# where focus goes, energy flows.

## today
I am grateful for

## 3
### Morning

01

02

03

Date

# 6
## Afternoon

01

02

03

04

05

06

# 9
## Night

01

02

03

04

05

06

07

08

09

The Universe is Listening

# where focus goes, energy flows.

## today
I am grateful for

## 3
Morning

01

02

03

Date

# 6
## Afternoon

01

02

03

04

05

06

# 9
## Night

01

02

03

04

05

06

07

08

09

The Universe is Listening

# where focus goes, energy flows.

## today
I am grateful for

## 3
Morning

01

02

03

Date _____

# 6
## Afternoon

01

02

03

04

05

06

# 9
## Night

01

02

03

04

05

06

07

08

09

The Universe is Listening

# where focus goes, energy flows.

## today
I am grateful for

## 3
Morning

01

02

03

Date

# 6
## Afternoon

01

02

03

04

05

06

# 9
## Night

01

02

03

04

05

06

07

08

09

The Universe is Listening

# where focus goes, energy flows.

## today

I am grateful for

## 3
Morning

01

02

03

Date

# 6
## Afternoon

01

02

03

04

05

06

# 9
## Night

01

02

03

04

05

06

07

08

09

The Universe is Listening

# where focus goes, energy flows.

## today
I am grateful for

## 3
Morning

01

02

03

Date

# 6
## Afternoon

- 01
- 02
- 03
- 04
- 05
- 06

# 9
## Night

- 01
- 02
- 03
- 04
- 05
- 06
- 07
- 08
- 09

The Universe is Listening

# where focus goes, energy flows.

## today

I am grateful for

## 3
Morning

01

02

03

Date

# 6
## Afternoon

01

02

03

04

05

06

# 9
## Night

01

02

03

04

05

06

07

08

09

The Universe is Listening

# where focus goes, energy flows.

## today
I am grateful for

## 3
Morning

01

02

03

Date

# 6
## Afternoon

01

02

03

04

05

06

# 9
## Night

01

02

03

04

05

06

07

08

09

# where focus goes, energy flows.

## today
I am grateful for

## 3
Morning

01

02

03

Date

# 6
## Afternoon

01

02

03

04

05

06

# 9
## Night

01

02

03

04

05

06

07

08

09

The Universe is Listening

# where focus goes, energy flows.

## today
I am grateful for

## 3
### Morning

01

02

03

Date

# 6
## Afternoon

01

02

03

04

05

06

# 9
## Night

01

02

03

04

05

06

07

08

09

The Universe is Listening

# where focus goes, energy flows.

## today
I am grateful for

## 3
Morning

01

02

03

Date

# 6
## Afternoon

01

02

03

04

05

06

# 9
## Night

01

02

03

04

05

06

07

08

09

The Universe is Listening

# where focus goes, energy flows.

## today
I am grateful for

|  |
|--|
|  |

## 3
Morning

| |
|--|
| 01 |
| 02 |
| 03 |

Date _____

# 6
## Afternoon

01

02

03

04

05

06

# 9
## Night

01

02

03

04

05

06

07

08

09

The Universe is Listening

# where focus goes, energy flows.

## today
I am grateful for

## 3
Morning

01

02

03

Date

# 6
## Afternoon

01

02

03

04

05

06

# 9
## Night

01

02

03

04

05

06

07

08

09

The Universe is Listening

# where focus goes, energy flows.

## today

I am grateful for

## 3
Morning

01

02

03

Date

# 6
## Afternoon

01

02

03

04

05

06

# 9
## Night

01

02

03

04

05

06

07

08

09

The Universe is Listening

# where focus goes, energy flows.

## today

I am grateful for

## 3
### Morning

01

02

03

Date

# 6
## Afternoon

01

02

03

04

05

06

# 9
## Night

01

02

03

04

05

06

07

08

09

The Universe is Listening

# where focus goes, energy flows.

## today

I am grateful for

## 3
Morning

01

02

03

Date

# 6
## Afternoon

01

02

03

04

05

06

# 9
## Night

01

02

03

04

05

06

07

08

09

The Universe is Listening

# where focus goes, energy flows.

## today
I am grateful for

## 3
Morning

01

02

03

Date

# 6
## Afternoon

01

02

03

04

05

06

# 9
## Night

01

02

03

04

05

06

07

08

09

The Universe is Listening

# where focus goes, energy flows.

## today
I am grateful for

## 3
Morning

01

02

03

Date

# 6
## Afternoon

01

02

03

04

05

06

# 9
## Night

01

02

03

04

05

06

07

08

09

The Universe is Listening

# where focus goes, energy flows.

## today
I am grateful for

## 3
Morning

01

02

03

Date

# 6
## Afternoon

01

02

03

04

05

06

# 9
## Night

01

02

03

04

05

06

07

08

09

The Universe is Listening

# where focus goes, energy flows.

## today

I am grateful for

## 3
Morning

01

02

03

Date

# 6
## Afternoon

01

02

03

04

05

06

# 9
## Night

01

02

03

04

05

06

07

08

09

The Universe is Listening

# where focus goes, energy flows.

## today
I am grateful for

## 3
Morning

01

02

03

Date

# 6
## Afternoon

01

02

03

04

05

06

# 9
## Night

01

02

03

04

05

06

07

08

09

The Universe is Listening

# where focus goes, energy flows.

## today
I am grateful for

## 3
Morning

01

02

03

Date

# 6
## Afternoon

01

02

03

04

05

06

# 9
## Night

01

02

03

04

05

06

07

08

09

The Universe is Listening

# where focus goes, energy flows.

## today
I am grateful for

## 3
Morning

01

02

03

Date

# 6
## Afternoon

01

02

03

04

05

06

# 9
## Night

01

02

03

04

05

06

07

08

09

The Universe is Listening

# where focus goes, energy flows.

## today
I am grateful for

## 3
Morning

01

02

03

Date

# 6
## Afternoon

01

02

03

04

05

06

# 9
## Night

01

02

03

04

05

06

07

08

09

The Universe is Listening

# where focus goes, energy flows.

## today

I am grateful for

|  |
|--|
|  |

## 3
### Morning

| |
|--|
| 01 |
| 02 |
| 03 |

Date

# 6
## Afternoon

01

02

03

04

05

06

# 9
## Night

01

02

03

04

05

06

07

08

09

The Universe is Listening

# where focus goes, energy flows.

## today
I am grateful for

## 3
Morning

01

02

03

Date

# 6
## Afternoon

01

02

03

04

05

06

# 9
## Night

01

02

03

04

05

06

07

08

09

The Universe is Listening

# where focus goes, energy flows.

## today
I am grateful for

## 3
Morning

01

02

03

Date

# 6
## Afternoon

01

02

03

04

05

06

# 9
## Night

01

02

03

04

05

06

07

08

09

The Universe is Listening

# where focus goes, energy flows.

## today

I am grateful for

## 3
Morning

01

02

03

Date

# 6
## Afternoon

01

02

03

04

05

06

# 9
## Night

01

02

03

04

05

06

07

08

09

The Universe is Listening

# where focus goes, energy flows.

## today
**I am grateful for**

## 3
**Morning**

01

02

03

Date

# 6
## Afternoon

01

02

03

04

05

06

# 9
## Night

01

02

03

04

05

06

07

08

09

The Universe is Listening

# where focus goes, energy flows.

## today
I am grateful for

|  |
|--|
|  |

## 3
Morning

| |
|--|
| 01 |
| 02 |
| 03 |

Date

# 6
## Afternoon

01

02

03

04

05

06

# 9
## Night

01

02

03

04

05

06

07

08

09

The Universe is Listening

# where focus goes, energy flows.

## today
I am grateful for

## 3
Morning

01

02

03

Date

# 6
## Afternoon

01

02

03

04

05

06

# 9
## Night

01

02

03

04

05

06

07

08

09

**The Universe is Listening**

# where focus goes, energy flows.

## today
I am grateful for

## 3
Morning

01

02

03

Date

# 6
## Afternoon

01

02

03

04

05

06

# 9
## Night

01

02

03

04

05

06

07

08

09

The Universe is Listening

# where focus goes, energy flows.

## today
I am grateful for

## 3
Morning

01

02

03

Date

# 6
## Afternoon

01

02

03

04

05

06

# 9
## Night

01

02

03

04

05

06

07

08

09

The Universe is Listening

# where focus goes, energy flows.

## today
I am grateful for

## 3
Morning

01

02

03

Date

# 6
## Afternoon

01

02

03

04

05

06

# 9
## Night

01

02

03

04

05

06

07

08

09

The Universe is Listening

# where focus goes, energy flows.

## today
I am grateful for

## 3
Morning

01

02

03

Date

# 6
## Afternoon

01

02

03

04

05

06

# 9
## Night

01

02

03

04

05

06

07

08

09

The Universe is Listening

# where focus goes, energy flows.

## today
I am grateful for

## 3
Morning

01

02

03

Date

# 6
## Afternoon

01

02

03

04

05

06

# 9
## Night

01

02

03

04

05

06

07

08

09

The Universe is Listening

# where focus goes, energy flows.

## today

I am grateful for

## 3
### Morning

01

02

03

Date

# 6
## Afternoon

01

02

03

04

05

06

# 9
## Night

01

02

03

04

05

06

07

08

09

The Universe is Listening

# where focus goes, energy flows.

## today

**I am grateful for**

## 3
### Morning

01

02

03

Date

# 6
## Afternoon

01

02

03

04

05

06

# 9
## Night

01

02

03

04

05

06

07

08

09

The Universe is Listening

# where focus goes, energy flows.

## today
I am grateful for

## 3
Morning

01

02

03

Date

# 6
## Afternoon

01

02

03

04

05

06

# 9
## Night

01

02

03

04

05

06

07

08

09

**The Universe is Listening**

# where focus goes, energy flows.

## today

I am grateful for

## 3
Morning

01

02

03

Date

# 6
## Afternoon

01

02

03

04

05

06

# 9
## Night

01

02

03

04

05

06

07

08

09

**The Universe is Listening**

# where focus goes, energy flows.

## today
I am grateful for

## 3
### Morning

01

02

03

Date

# 6
## Afternoon

01

02

03

04

05

06

# 9
## Night

01

02

03

04

05

06

07

08

09

The Universe is Listening

# where focus goes, energy flows.

## today
I am grateful for

## 3
Morning

01

02

03

Date

# 6
## Afternoon

01

02

03

04

05

06

# 9
## Night

01

02

03

04

05

06

07

08

09

The Universe is Listening

# where focus goes, energy flows.

## today
I am grateful for

## 3
Morning

01

02

03

Date

# 6
## Afternoon

01

02

03

04

05

06

# 9
## Night

01

02

03

04

05

06

07

08

09

The Universe is Listening

# where focus goes, energy flows.

## today
I am grateful for

## 3
Morning

01

02

03

Date

# 6
## Afternoon

01

02

03

04

05

06

# 9
## Night

01

02

03

04

05

06

07

08

09

The Universe is Listening

# where focus goes, energy flows.

## today
I am grateful for

## 3
Morning

01

02

03

Date

# 6
## Afternoon

01

02

03

04

05

06

# 9
## Night

01

02

03

04

05

06

07

08

09

The Universe is Listening

# where focus goes, energy flows.

## today

I am grateful for

## 3
Morning

01

02

03

Date

# 6
## Afternoon

01

02

03

04

05

06

# 9
## Night

01

02

03

04

05

06

07

08

09

The Universe is Listening

# where focus goes, energy flows.

## today
I am grateful for

## 3
Morning

01

02

03

Date

# 6
## Afternoon

01

02

03

04

05

06

# 9
## Night

01

02

03

04

05

06

07

08

09

The Universe is Listening

# where focus goes, energy flows.

## today
I am grateful for

 

## 3
Morning

01

02

03

Date _____

# 6
## Afternoon

01

02

03

04

05

06

# 9
## Night

01

02

03

04

05

06

07

08

09

The Universe is Listening

# where focus goes, energy flows.

## today
**I am grateful for**

## 3
**Morning**

01

02

03

Date

# 6
## Afternoon

01

02

03

04

05

06

# 9
## Night

01

02

03

04

05

06

07

08

09

The Universe is Listening

# where focus goes, energy flows.

## today

I am grateful for

## 3
### Morning

01

02

03

Date

# 6
## Afternoon

01

02

03

04

05

06

# 9
## Night

01

02

03

04

05

06

07

08

09

The Universe is Listening

# where focus goes, energy flows.

## today
I am grateful for

## 3
Morning

01

02

03

Date

# 6
## Afternoon

01

02

03

04

05

06

# 9
## Night

01

02

03

04

05

06

07

08

09

The Universe is Listening

# where focus goes, energy flows.

## today

I am grateful for

## 3
Morning

01

02

03

Date

# 6
## Afternoon

01

02

03

04

05

06

# 9
## Night

01

02

03

04

05

06

07

08

09

The Universe is Listening

# where focus goes, energy flows.

## today
I am grateful for

## 3
Morning

01

02

03

Date

# 6
## Afternoon

01

02

03

04

05

06

# 9
## Night

01

02

03

04

05

06

07

08

09

The Universe is Listening

# where focus goes, energy flows.

## today
I am grateful for

## 3
Morning

01

02

03

Date

# 6
## Afternoon

01

02

03

04

05

06

# 9
## Night

01

02

03

04

05

06

07

08

09

The Universe is Listening

# where focus goes, energy flows.

## today

I am grateful for

### 3
Morning

01

02

03

Date

# 6
## Afternoon

01

02

03

04

05

06

# 9
## Night

01

02

03

04

05

06

07

08

09

# where focus goes, energy flows.

## today

**I am grateful for**

## 3
**Morning**

01

02

03

Date

# 6
## Afternoon

01

02

03

04

05

06

# 9
## Night

01

02

03

04

05

06

07

08

09

The Universe is Listening

# where focus goes, energy flows.

## today
I am grateful for

|  |
|---|
|  |

## 3
Morning

|  |
|---|
| 01 |
| 02 |
| 03 |

Date

# 6
## Afternoon

01

02

03

04

05

06

# 9
## Night

01

02

03

04

05

06

07

08

09

# where focus goes, energy flows.

## today
I am grateful for

## 3
Morning

01

02

03

Date

# 6
## Afternoon

01

02

03

04

05

06

# 9
## Night

01

02

03

04

05

06

07

08

09

The Universe is Listening

# where focus goes, energy flows.

## today
I am grateful for

## 3
Morning

01

02

03

Date

# 6
## Afternoon

01

02

03

04

05

06

# 9
## Night

01

02

03

04

05

06

07

08

09

The Universe is Listening

# where focus goes, energy flows.

## today
I am grateful for

## 3
Morning

01

02

03

Date

# 6
## Afternoon

01

02

03

04

05

06

# 9
## Night

01

02

03

04

05

06

07

08

09

The Universe is Listening

# where focus goes, energy flows.

## today
I am grateful for

## 3
Morning

01

02

03

Date

# 6
## Afternoon

01

02

03

04

05

06

# 9
## Night

01

02

03

04

05

06

07

08

09

The Universe is Listening

# where focus goes, energy flows.

## today
I am grateful for

## 3
Morning

01

02

03

Date

# 6
## Afternoon

01

02

03

04

05

06

# 9
## Night

01

02

03

04

05

06

07

08

09

The Universe is Listening

# where focus goes, energy flows.

## today
I am grateful for

|  |
|---|
|  |

## 3
Morning

| |
|---|
| 01 |
| 02 |
| 03 |

Date

# 6
## Afternoon

01

02

03

04

05

06

# 9
## Night

01

02

03

04

05

06

07

08

09

# where focus goes, energy flows.

## today
I am grateful for

## 3
Morning

01

02

03

Date

# 6
## Afternoon

01

02

03

04

05

06

# 9
## Night

01

02

03

04

05

06

07

08

09

The Universe is Listening

# where focus goes, energy flows.

## today
I am grateful for

## 3
Morning

01

02

03

Date

# 6
## Afternoon

01

02

03

04

05

06

# 9
## Night

01

02

03

04

05

06

07

08

09

# where focus goes, energy flows.

## today
I am grateful for

## 3
Morning

01

02

03

Date

# 6
## Afternoon

01

02

03

04

05

06

# 9
## Night

01

02

03

04

05

06

07

08

09

# where focus goes, energy flows.

## today

I am grateful for

## 3
### Morning

01

02

03

Date

# 6
## Afternoon

01

02

03

04

05

06

# 9
## Night

01

02

03

04

05

06

07

08

09

**The Universe is Listening**

# where focus goes, energy flows.

## today

**I am grateful for**

 

## 3
### Morning

01

02

03

Date

# 6
## Afternoon

01

02

03

04

05

06

# 9
## Night

01

02

03

04

05

06

07

08

09

The Universe is Listening

# where focus goes, energy flows.

## today
I am grateful for

## 3
Morning

01

02

03

Date

# 6
## Afternoon

01

02

03

04

05

06

# 9
## Night

01

02

03

04

05

06

07

08

09

The Universe is Listening

# where focus goes, energy flows.

## today
I am grateful for

## 3
Morning

01

02

03

Date

# 6
## Afternoon

01

02

03

04

05

06

# 9
## Night

01

02

03

04

05

06

07

08

09

The Universe is Listening

# where focus goes, energy flows.

## today
I am grateful for

## 3
Morning

01

02

03

Date

# 6
## Afternoon

01

02

03

04

05

06

# 9
## Night

01

02

03

04

05

06

07

08

09

The Universe is Listening

# where focus goes, energy flows.

## today
I am grateful for

## 3
Morning

01

02

03

Date

# 6
## Afternoon

01

02

03

04

05

06

# 9
## Night

01

02

03

04

05

06

07

08

09

The Universe is Listening

# where focus goes, energy flows.

## today
I am grateful for

## 3
Morning

01

02

03

Date

# 6
## Afternoon

01

02

03

04

05

06

# 9
## Night

01

02

03

04

05

06

07

08

09

**The Universe is Listening**

# where focus goes, energy flows.

## today

I am grateful for

## 3
### Morning

01

02

03

Date

# 6
## Afternoon

01

02

03

04

05

06

# 9
## Night

01

02

03

04

05

06

07

08

09

The Universe is Listening

# where focus goes, energy flows.

## today
I am grateful for

## 3
Morning

01

02

03

Date

# 6
## Afternoon

01

02

03

04

05

06

# 9
## Night

01

02

03

04

05

06

07

08

09

The Universe is Listening

# where focus goes, energy flows.

## today
I am grateful for

## 3
Morning

01

02

03

Date

# 6
## Afternoon

01

02

03

04

05

06

# 9
## Night

01

02

03

04

05

06

07

08

09

The Universe is Listening

# where focus goes, energy flows.

## today
I am grateful for

## 3
### Morning

01

02

03

Date

# 6
## Afternoon

01

02

03

04

05

06

# 9
## Night

01

02

03

04

05

06

07

08

09

The Universe is Listening

# where focus goes, energy flows.

## today
I am grateful for

## 3
### Morning

01

02

03

Date

# 6
## Afternoon

01

02

03

04

05

06

# 9
## Night

01

02

03

04

05

06

07

08

09

The Universe is Listening

# where focus goes, energy flows.

## today
I am grateful for

## 3
Morning

01

02

03

Date

# 6
## Afternoon

01

02

03

04

05

06

# 9
## Night

01

02

03

04

05

06

07

08

09

The Universe is Listening

# where focus goes, energy flows.

## today

I am grateful for

## 3
Morning

01

02

03

Date

# 6
## Afternoon

01

02

03

04

05

06

# 9
## Night

01

02

03

04

05

06

07

08

09

The Universe is Listening

# where focus goes, energy flows.

## today
I am grateful for

## 3
Morning

01

02

03

Date

# 6
## Afternoon

01

02

03

04

05

06

# 9
## Night

01

02

03

04

05

06

07

08

09

The Universe is Listening

# where focus goes, energy flows.

## today

I am grateful for

## 3
### Morning

01

02

03

Date

# 6
## Afternoon

01

02

03

04

05

06

# 9
## Night

01

02

03

04

05

06

07

08

09

The Universe is Listening

# where focus goes, energy flows.

## today
I am grateful for

## 3
Morning

01

02

03

Date

# 6
## Afternoon

01

02

03

04

05

06

# 9
## Night

01

02

03

04

05

06

07

08

09

The Universe is Listening

# where focus goes, energy flows.

## today
I am grateful for

|  |
|--|
|  |

## 3
Morning

| |
|--|
| 01 |
| 02 |
| 03 |

Date _____

# 6
## Afternoon

01

02

03

04

05

06

# 9
## Night

01

02

03

04

05

06

07

08

09

The Universe is Listening

# where focus goes, energy flows.

## today
I am grateful for

## 3
Morning

01

02

03

Date

# 6
## Afternoon

01

02

03

04

05

06

# 9
## Night

01

02

03

04

05

06

07

08

09

The Universe is Listening

# where focus goes, energy flows.

## today

I am grateful for

### 3
Morning

01

02

03

Date

# 6
## Afternoon

01

02

03

04

05

06

# 9
## Night

01

02

03

04

05

06

07

08

09

The Universe is Listening

# where focus goes, energy flows.

## today
I am grateful for

## 3
Morning

01

02

03

Date

# 6
## Afternoon

01

02

03

04

05

06

# 9
## Night

01

02

03

04

05

06

07

08

09

The Universe is Listening

# where focus goes, energy flows.

## today

I am grateful for

## 3
### Morning

01

02

03

Date

# 6
## Afternoon

01

02

03

04

05

06

# 9
## Night

01

02

03

04

05

06

07

08

09

The Universe is Listening

# where focus goes, energy flows.

## today
I am grateful for

## 3
Morning

01

02

03

Date

# 6
## Afternoon

01

02

03

04

05

06

# 9
## Night

01

02

03

04

05

06

07

08

09

The Universe is Listening

# where focus goes, energy flows.

## today
I am grateful for

## 3
Morning

01

02

03

Date

# 6
## Afternoon

01

02

03

04

05

06

# 9
## Night

01

02

03

04

05

06

07

08

09

The Universe is Listening

# where focus goes, energy flows.

## today
I am grateful for

## 3
Morning

01

02

03

Date

# 6
## Afternoon

01

02

03

04

05

06

# 9
## Night

01

02

03

04

05

06

07

08

09

The Universe is Listening

# where focus goes, energy flows.

## today

I am grateful for

### 3
Morning

01

02

03

Date

# 6
## Afternoon

01

02

03

04

05

06

# 9
## Night

01

02

03

04

05

06

07

08

09

The Universe is Listening

# where focus goes, energy flows.

## today
I am grateful for

## 3
Morning

01

02

03

Date

# 6
## Afternoon

01

02

03

04

05

06

# 9
## Night

01

02

03

04

05

06

07

08

09

The Universe is Listening

# 96
Days
___

## daily progress check

| | | | | | |
|---|---|---|---|---|---|
| 01 | 02 | 03 | 04 | 05 | 06 |
| 07 | 08 | 09 | 10 | 11 | 12 |
| 13 | 14 | 15 | 16 | 17 | 18 |
| 19 | 20 | 21 | 22 | 23 | 24 |
| 25 | 26 | 27 | 28 | 29 | 30 |
| 31 | 32 | 33 | 34 | 35 | 36 |
| 37 | 38 | 39 | 40 | 41 | 42 |
| 43 | 44 | 45 | 46 | 47 | 48 |

💡 **Quick tip:** *Bookmark this page!*

| | | | | | | |
|---|---|---|---|---|---|---|
| 49 | 50 | 51 | 52 | 53 | 54 |
| 55 | 56 | 57 | 58 | 59 | 60 |
| 61 | 62 | 63 | 64 | 65 | 66 |
| 67 | 68 | 69 | 70 | 71 | 72 |
| 73 | 74 | 75 | 76 | 77 | 78 |
| 79 | 80 | 81 | 82 | 83 | 84 |
| 85 | 86 | 87 | 88 | 89 | 90 |
| 91 | 92 | 93 | 94 | 95 | 96 |

The Universe is Listening

💡 **Quick tip:** *Bookmark this page!*

# positive affirmations.

Positive affirmations teach us to love ourselves. They are optimistic phrases centered around generosity, patience, and kindness.

Read these mantras and feel the kind words soak into your soul. Believe them and watch their power manifest in your daily life.

*I trust the Universe. It gives me exactly what I need at exactly the right time.*

———

*Everything works out perfectly for me. I am creating my dream life.*

———

*I am worthy of receiving my yes. Now release everything that is not serving my highest purpose.*

———

*I'm worthy enough to follow my dreams and manifest my desires.*

———

*My business gets better and better every day.*

*I work where I want, when I want, and with people I want to work with.*

———

*I am abundant in my finances, in happiness, and in love.*

———

*My soul is ready to live the life of my dreams.*

———

*I am wealthy and prosperous in every aspect of my life.*

———

*I surround myself with positive and genuine people who help me and encourage me to reach my goals.*

———

*The Universe always has my back.*

*I now release any fears or limiting beliefs I may have about achieving my yes.*

―――

*Every day I am moving towards my best life.*

―――

*I am smart, creative, and motivated. I only take yes for an answer.*

―――

*My intentions for my life are clear. What I am seeking is seeking me.*

―――

*I'm creating a life of passion and purpose.*

―――

*There is no place for negative self-talk in my life. I am completely and utterly in love with myself.*

*It is OK for me to have everything I want. Every day I move towards having everything I want.*

―――

*I step out of my comfort zone to achieve my goals and find comfort in change and new environments as I move towards my yes.*

―――

*I love, support, and believe in myself.*

The Universe is Listening

💡 **Quick tip:** *Bookmark this page!*

# manifestation quotes.

"Ask for what you want and be prepared to get it."

– Maya Angelou

———

"Imagination is everything. It is the preview of life's coming attractions."

– Albert Einstein

———

"Once you make a decision, the universe conspires to make it happen."

– Ralph Waldo Emerson

———

"Destiny is not a matter of chance, it is a matter of choice."

– William Jennings Bryan

———

"The universe is not outside of you. Look inside yourself; everything that you want, you already are."

– Rumi

"Our intention is everything. Nothing happens on this planet without it. Not one single thing has ever been accomplished without intention."

– Jim Carrey

---

"Whatever you can do, or dream, you can, begin it. Boldness has genius, power, and magic in it. Begin it now."

– Johann Wolfgang Von Goethe

---

"When your primary function is to be happy, then whatever comes to you is irrelevant. Happiness is your true manifestation."

– Gabrielle Bernstein

---

"The greatest discovery of my generation is that human beings can alter their lives by altering their attitudes of mind."

– William James

"Every single second is an opportunity to change your life because in any moment you can change the way you feel."

– Rhonda Byrne

―――

Keep your thoughts positive because your thoughts become your words. Keep your words positive because your words become your behavior. Keep your behavior positive because your behavior becomes your habits. Keep your habits positive because your habits become your values. Keep your values positive because your values become your destiny."

– Gandhi

―――

"Be thankful for what you have, you'll end up having more. If you concentrate on what you don't have, you will never ever have enough."

– Oprah Winfrey

―――

"A person is what he or she thinks about all day long."

– Ralph Waldo Emerson

*"Every great work, every big accomplishment, has been brought into manifestation through holding to the vision, and often just before the big achievement, comes apparent failure and discouragement."*

– Jim Carrey

———

*"Eliminate all doubt and replace it with the full expectation that you will receive what you are asking for."*

– Rhonda Byrne

———

*"Your mind is a powerful magnet that will attract to you the things you identify yourself with. If you have sad thoughts, you will attract tragedies. If you are a good man, you will attract the company of good people."*

– Alfredo Karras

"What you radiate outward in your thoughts, feelings, mental pictures and words, you attract into your life."

– Catherine Ponder

———

"To be happy with yourself in the present moment while maintaining a dream of your future is a grand recipe for manifestation. When you feel so whole that you no longer care whether "it" will happen, that's when amazing things materialize before your eyes."

– Joe Dispenza

———

"Go confidently in the direction of your dreams. Live the life you have imagined."

– Henry David Thoreau

The Universe is Listening

# your manifesting toolkit.

### Use a vision board

Vision boarding is something we do organically as a child and teenager. We surround ourselves with pictures and posters of what we want to be or do. We do this because **seeing our dream future and being excited by its prospect is an incredible tool.** It raises our vibration and changes our thought patterns.

To make a vision board, choose a journal that you will revisit or a spot in your wall that you often look at. Fill it with pictures that illustrate the future you want. It could be a picture of your dream house, your perfect holiday, a pregnant stomach, your ideal wedding dress. Take your time finding these pictures.
Each photo should send a bolt of excitement and empowerment through you. By surrounding yourself with these, you can begin subconsciously manifesting each time you see them.

## Manifest with crystals

———

Crystals are thousands, if not millions, of years old. Formed by hardened magma, people have recognized the power of crystals for thousands of years. Research shows Ancient Sumerians used them for healing dating back to 2000 BC. The Ancient Egyptians also used crystals such as lazuli and clear quartz for protection and health.

**Crystals possess potent energies that influence the vibrations around us.** Set intentions into your crystals by speaking your affirmation while holding them. Focus on the connections between your words, your belief, and the crystal. Each time you hold the crystal, feel the weight of that belief.

**Different crystals work best for different things. Here are a few examples:**

- ***Citrine*** is a well-known manifesting powerhouse. It's potent for attracting wealth.

- ***Clear quartz*** amplifies your intentions. You can use it to strengthen any manifestation.

- ***Rose quartz*** is remarkable at attracting love.

- ***Carnelian*** is best for manifesting creativity and motivation.

- ***Amethyst*** is incredible for manifesting healing, wisdom, tranquillity and clarity.

# conclusion.

**When you feel good and focus on feeling good, more good things come.**

This is not an astonishing miracle; this is science. You are matching the frequency of what you desire, and the universe delivers. It's a concoction of deliberate intentions that paint the canvas of your reality. Simply put, your life is a manifestation of your thoughts, and you can create your reality through mere thinking.

Use the power of this book and the 369 method to decide on what you want, intentionally manifest it, and patiently wait for the universe to deliver. It requires believing wholeheartedly in what you are asking for and waiting for the universe to make it happen in the most remarkable and often unexpected way.

**The power of this science and technique is in your hands.**

# take hold of it and transform your life.

Copyright © 2021

All rights reserved. No part of this book may be reproduced or used in any manner without the prior written permission of the copyright owner, except for the use of brief quotations in a book review.

**Written by**
David Rooney & Ruby Nyika

**Design by**
Renee Landers

Printed in Great Britain
by Amazon